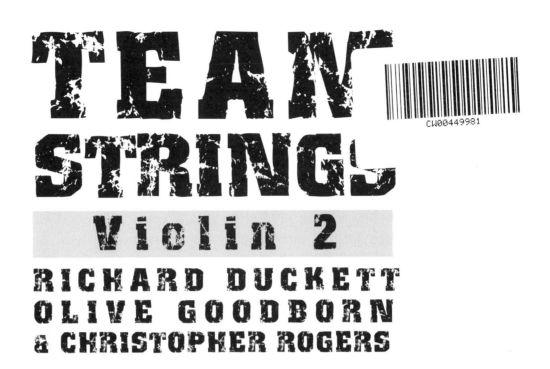

TEAM STRINGS

Violin 2

RICHARD DUCKETT
OLIVE GOODBORN
& CHRISTOPHER ROGERS

Edited by Barrie Carson Turner

First published in 2002 by International Music Publications Ltd
This edition © 2011 by Faber Music Ltd
This edition first published in 2011 by Faber Music Ltd
Bloomsbury House 74–77 Great Russell Street London WC1B 3DA
Cover photography by Keven Erickson
Cover design by Susan Clarke
Instruments photographed by kind permission of Yamaha-Kemble Music (UK) Ltd
Music engraving and typesetting by Barnes Music Engraving Ltd
Printed in England by Caligraving Ltd

ISBN10: 0-571-52805-8
EAN13: 978-0-571-52805-9

To buy Faber Music publications or to find out about the full range of titles available
please contact your local music retailer or Faber Music sales enquiries:
Faber Music Ltd, Burnt Mill, Elizabeth Way, Harlow CM20 2HX
Tel: +44 (0) 1279 82 89 82   Fax: +44 (0) 1279 82 89 83
sales@fabermusic.com   fabermusic.com

FABER *ff* MUSIC

Edited by BARRIE CARSON TURNER

Piano accompaniments by BARRIE CARSON TURNER

INTERNATIONAL MUSIC PUBLICATIONS LIMITED would like to thank the following
publishers for permission to use arrangements of their copyright material in TEAM STRINGS 2.
HEIGH-HO – Music by Frank Churchill
© 1937 & 2002 Bourne Co, USA
Warner/Chappell Music Ltd, London W6 8BS
DAISY BELL – Words and Music by Harry Dacre
© 1893 & 2002 Francis Day & Hunter Ltd, London WC2H 0QY
I GOT RHYTHM – Music and Lyrics by George Gershwin and Ira Gershwin
© 1930 (renewed) & 2002 WB Music Corp, USA
Warner/Chappell Music Ltd, London W6 8BS
THE TEDDY BEARS' PICNIC – Music by John Bratton
© 1907 & 2002 M Witmark & Sons, USA
B Feldman & Co Ltd, London WC2H 0QY
OVER THE RAINBOW – Music by Harold Arlen
© 1938 & 2002 EMI Catalogue Partnership, EMI Feist Catalog Inc and EMI United Partnership Ltd, USA
Worldwide print rights controlled by Warner Bros Publications Inc/IMP Ltd
OH, LADY BE GOOD – Music and Lyrics by George Gershwin and Ira Gershwin
© 1924 (renewed) & 2002 WB Music Corp, USA
Warner/Chappell Music Ltd, London W6 8BS
THE NORTHERN LIGHTS OF OLD ABERDEEN – Music by Mary Webb
© 1952 & 2002 Kerrs Music Corp Ltd, Glasgow G3 7DZ
EDELWEISS – Music by Richard Rodgers
© 1959 Richard Rodgers and Oscar Hammerstein II
Copyright renewed
This arrangement © 2002 Williamson Music
Williamson Music owner of publication and allied rights throughout the world
LITTLE DONKEY – Words and Music by Eric Boswell
© 1959 & 2002 Chappell Music Ltd, London W6 8BS
POMP AND CIRCUMSTANCE MARCH NO. 1 IN D, OP. 39/1 – Music by Edward Elgar
© 1901 & 2002 Boosey & Co. Ltd
Reprinted by permission of Boosey & Hawkes Music Publishers Ltd.
BLOWIN' IN THE WIND – Words and Music by Bob Dylan
© 1962 & 2002 Warner Bros. Inc.,
Copyright renewed 1990 Special Rider Music.
International copyright secured. All rights reserved.
Reprinted by permission of Music Sales Corporation.
SUMMERTIME – Music and Lyrics by Geoge Gershwin, Du Bose and Dorothy Heyward and Ira Gershwin
© 1935 (renewed 1962) & 2002 George Gershwin Music, Ira Gershwin Music and Du Bose and Dorothy Heyward Memorial Fund
All rights administered by WB Music Corp, USA
Warner/Chappell Music Ltd, London W6 8BS
STAR WARS (MAIN TITLE) – Music by John Williams
© 1984 & 2002 Bantha Music, USA
Warner/Chappell Music Ltd, London W6 8BS
MY HEART WILL GO ON – Music by James Horner
© 1997 & 2002 T C F Music Publishing Inc., Fox Film Music Corporation, Blue Sky Rider Songs and Irving Music Inc, USA
Worldwide print rights controlled by Warner Bros Publications Inc/IMP Ltd and Rondor Music (London) Ltd, London W6 8JA
PINK PANTHER – Music by Henry Mancini
© 1964 & 2002 Northridge Music Inc, EMI Catalogue Partnership, EMI U Catalog Inc and
EMI United Partnership Ltd, USA
Worldwide print rights controlled by Warner Bros Publications Inc/IMP Ltd

Sincere thanks are extended to the following people:
CHRISTOPHER BULL, author and arranger of ensemble TEAM STRINGS BOOK 1, for the original plan for TEAM STRINGS BOOK 2.
CELIA DOUBLEDAY, cellist, who worked on the material in preparation.
ANN GOODBORN, double bass tutor who worked with Christopher Bull on ideas for the original draft.
MONICA HERMOLLE, cellist, for her invaluable support in the preparation of these books.
BRIAN LESTER, Birmingham Instrumental Team, for his invaluable advise and support.
SHELAGH REID, violinist and teacher (Aberdeen), for her invaluable advise on technical matters and repertoire.
JENNY SMITH, violinist and teacher (Worcestershire), for her invaluable advise and support.
LORNA WINDASS, violinist and teacher (Addenburgh, Oxfordshire), for her invaluable support and help on bowing the material.

CD track listing

Each track includes two bars of clicks to bring you in.

	track	page
Violin tuning notes	1	–
Viola tuning notes	2	–
Cello tuning notes	3	–
Double bass tuning notes	4	–
Abschied	25	28
Acapulco Bay	35	44
Au clair de la lune	34	43
Auld lang syne	44	58
Believe me, if all those endearing young charms	33	41
Blowin' in the wind	42	53
Camptown races	30	36
Caribbean dance	40	49
Country gardens	24	27
Coventry carol	47	61
Daisy bell	7	5
Eternal Father	51	65
Heigh-ho	6	4
Hoe down	45	59
I got rhythm	21	24
I know the Lord's laid his hands on me	39	48
I saw three ships	19	22
Joy to the world	20	23
Little donkey	41	51
Liza Jane	38	47
Loch Lomond	17	21
Lullaby	36	45

	track	page
Lullaby (Brahms)	16	19
Marie's wedding	31	38
My bonnie lies over the ocean	8	7
My grandfather's clock	5	2
My heart will go on	50	64
New world symphony	13	18
O little town of Bethlehem	37	46
Oh! Susannah	29	34
Oh, lady be good!	27	32
Over the rainbow	26	30
Pink panther	52	66
Sailor's song	12	17
Scotland the brave	18	21
Shortnin' bread	43	56
Soldier, soldier	9	10
Star wars	49	62
Summertime	48	61
Swing low, sweet chariot	15	19
Take it away, man	11	15
The girl I left behind me	32	39
The rowan tree	14	19
The teddy bears' picnic	23	27
The truth from above	46	60
This train	10	14
Waltz from The merry widow	28	34
When the saints go marching in	22	25

Team Strings 2 Ensemble

TEAM STRINGS 2 ensemble material has been specially written so that it can be played by almost any combination of string instruments the teacher may encounter.

On each ensemble page there are three or four parts. The first is the melody and the second is a duet part. The third and fourth parts are either a bass line, a harmony part or a descant. Each piece can therefore be used as a solo, duet, trio, or quartet with or without piano accompaniment.

By allocating the parts to different instruments it is easy to create a considerable variety of mixed ensembles, from a simple duet to a full string orchestra.

Each piece which can be played in emsemble or with a piano accompaniment also has the option of a CD backing track.

In addition to this, each piece can be extended into a longer one by varying the textures in subsequent verses. This can be done by reallocating the parts, playing in unison, using pizzicato accompaniments, introducing solo passages, etc.

The following symbols have been used to provide an immediate visual identification:

  Pieces with piano accompaniment

  Ensemble page
(score included in ACCOMPANIMENTS book)

  Pieces which appear in the same place on the same page in all four TEAM STRINGS 2 books

Vln	Vla	Vc	Db

The box to the left of each arrangement or score indicates where each piece can be found in the solo instrumental books.

Introducing Team Strings 2

As in TEAM STRINGS, TEAM STRINGS 2 has been designed to meet the needs of young string players everywhere, whether lessons are given individually, in groups or in the classroom.

Musical variety

TEAM STRINGS 2 has been specially designed to follow the original TEAM STRINGS TUTOR, although it can be used to follow on from any beginner string book. It offers the same wide variety of musical styles as the original, but is further enhanced by titles from the world of jazz and blues supported by a three-part course of improvisation techniques.

Ensemble pieces

TEAM STRINGS 2 offers corresponding pages of music which can be played in harmony for mixed string ensembles, from duet right up to full string orchestra. From page 43 onwards, TEAM STRINGS 2, TEAM BRASS, PERCUSSION and WOODWIND naturally share much of the same ensemble material allowing it to develop into full orchestra. As the TEAM STRINGS 2 tutors contain 25 pages of ensemble, they are suitable for school orchestra, string orchestra, symphony orchestra as well as solo, duet and other small groups.

Flexible course

TEAM STRINGS 2 does not offer guidance on how to play or teach a string instrument but rather offers material which the professional teacher can use to structure courses for individual pupils.

National Curriculum & GCSE skills

TEAM STRINGS 2 has been designed to help meet the requirements of the National Curriculum for music. In addition to fostering musical literacy, 'Play By Ear' lines provide early opportunities for composition and improvisation. This aspect of TEAM STRINGS can be a useful starting point for these elements in the GCSE examination course now followed by secondary schools.

Comprehensive notes on the use of this series, scores of the ensemble material, piano accompaniments and approaches to creative music making are given in the accompaniments book.

Accompaniments

Accompaniments for selected solo pieces, and the ensemble pieces, are available in the Accompaniments book and on the CD.

Lesson diary and practice chart

Date (week commencing)	Enter number of minutes practised							Teacher indicates which pages to study
	Mon	Tue	Wed	Thu	Fri	Sat	Sun	

My grandfather's clock

4 clicks intro

Words and Music by
HENRY CLAY WORK (1832–1884)

The four dots mean
you can repeat the music
as often as you want

Moderately

3.

Moderately

4.

* Chime effect. Repeat chord 12 times, ad lib., and hold.

Heigh-ho

Words by LARRY MORLEY
Music by FRANK E. CHURCHILL

7 clicks intro

Simple gifts

Shaker melody

Daisy Bell

Words and Music by
HARRY DACRE (1860–1922)

6 clicks intro

rall. (rallentando) means
gradually slowing down

If you're happy and you know it

Traditional

Oranges and lemons

Traditional

The Lincolnshire poacher

Traditional

Slur study

Key signature of
E minor

Melancholia

CHRISTOPHER BULL (1950–1994)

My Bonnie lies over the ocean

5 clicks intro

Traditional

With motion

1.

With motion

2.

With motion

3.

Staccato

Legato
means play the notes smoothly

Staccato
means play the notes short

Etude 1

Etude 2

Staccato duet

CHRISTOPHER BULL (1950–1994)

This sign means play the note pizzicato with your left hand

West Heath lilt

The cuckoo

EDWARD DUCKETT

Hornpipe

HENRY PURCELL (1659–1695)

Soldier, soldier

4 clicks intro

Traditional

1.

2.

Broken slurs

Das Blumchen wunderhold

LUDWIG VAN BEETHOVEN (1770–1827)

Sleigh ride

CHRISTOPHER BULL (1950–1994)

Study 1

German tune

Traditional

Study 2

Minuet in G

HENRY PURCELL (1659–1695)

Rhythmic decoration

Take it away man

4 clicks intro

Cockles and mussels

Traditional

Hoch Wass' kommt von draussen Rhein

Traditional

With a gentle rhythm

Fairly fast

Sailors' song

4 clicks intro

Traditional

Rhythmically

1.

7

13

Rhythmically

2.

7

13

Rhythmically

3.

7

13

Rhythmically

4.

7

13

The key of D major

Music in D major has a
key signature of TWO sharps

L. A. nitespot
Twelve bar blues

Lasst uns erfreuen

Chorale melody

New world symphony

4 clicks intro

ANTONIN DVOŘÁK (1841–1904)

The rowan tree

3 clicks intro

Traditional

Swing low, sweet chariot

4 clicks intro

Traditional

Lullaby

5 clicks intro

JOHANNES BRAHMS (1833–1897)

For (s)he's a jolly good fellow

Comin' thro' the rye

Traditional

Snappily

Loch Lomond

3 clicks intro

Calmly

Traditional

Scotland the brave

4 clicks intro

Like a march

Traditional

play by ear

Moderato

I saw three ships

4 ♩. clicks intro

Traditional

Joy to the world

4 clicks intro

GEORGE FREDERIC HANDEL (1685–1759)

Melodic improvisation

When the saints go marching in

Traditional

5 clicks intro

Medium swing

1.

After playing the tune you can
IMPROVISE over parts 2, 3 and 4

Medium swing

2.

Medium swing

3.

Medium swing

4.

The key of C major

Music in C major has a
key signature of no sharps or flats

Observe the rests if
playing with viola or cello

Scale and arpeggio of C major

Biddy Biddy

Traditional

Easy tempo

Look for scale
patterns

Round the scale

This means rest for 3 whole bars, so count ①2, ②2, ③2 and then play from bar 4

The teddy bears' picnic

JOHN W. BRATTON

Country gardens

4 clicks intro

Traditional

Summer is icumen in
Round

Traditional

Abschied

6 clicks intro

Traditional

Intervals

Study in C

Over the rainbow

4 clicks intro

Words by E. Y. HARBURG
Music by HAROLD ARLEN

Harmonics

Touch the notes lightly with the 4th finger to play the harmonics

Pearls

Using the 4th finger

This 4th finger makes the same sound as the E string

Step round

Whither blows the wind

CROTCHET TRIPLETS mean that three crotchets are played in the time of one minim

Play some of your tunes from Book 1 using 4th finger instead of open strings

Oh, Lady be good!

Music and Lyrics by
GEORGE GERSHWIN and IRA GERSHWIN

4 clicks intro

The keys of Canterbury

Allegretto

Traditional

Oh, how lovely is the evening

Round

Cantabile

Traditional

Polovtsian dance

Lilting, not fast

ALEXANDER BORODIN (1833–1887)

Barn dance

Waltz from The Merry Widow

FRANZ LEHÁR (1870–1948)

6 clicks intro

Oh! Susannah

STEPHEN C. FOSTER (1826–1864)

4 clicks intro

Scale and arpeggio of G major
(2 octaves)

Etude 1

Etude 2

Soliloquy

Caressingly

Flowing

Smoothly

Camptown races

STEPHEN C. FOSTER (1826–1864)

4 clicks intro

COL LEGNO means tap the strings with the wood of the bow

Hickory, dickory, dock!

Traditional

Col legno

Black Forest
Fits with *German Tune* in book 1, page 23

Summer's end
Fits with *Autumn* in book 1, page 21

Caribbean carnival
Fits with *Jamaican dance* in book 1, page 49

High B

Marie's wedding

4 clicks intro

Traditional

Cindy

Traditional

The girl I left behind me

4 clicks intro

Traditional

The northern lights of old Aberdeen

MARY WEBB

Hot cross buns

Decisively

Traditional

Key signature of
A minor

When Johnny comes marching home

Marziale

Traditional

God save the Queen

Nobly

Traditional

Believe me, if all those endearing charms

THOMAS MOORE (1779–1852)

5 ♪ clicks intro

The key of F major

The note B♭

Music in F major has a key signature of ONE flat

The FLAT lowers the pitch of a note by one semitone

Barcarolle

JACQUES OFFENBACH (1819–1880)

Slow waltz

Triste

Round

Make up your own tunes using the notes G, A, B♭, C and D

Edelweiss

Words by OSCAR HAMMERSTEIN II
Music by RICHARD RODGERS

Au clair de la lune

Fits with *Au clair de la lune* in Brass,
Woodwind and Percussion books (page 37)

4 clicks intro

Traditional

play by ear

Upper B♭

Acapulco Bay

Fits with *Acapulco Bay* in Flute and Oboe books (pages 6 and 7)

4 clicks intro

Tempo de beguine

Slur round

Fits with *Step round* in Flute and Oboe books (page 8)

Steady

Skip to my Lou

Traditional

Playfully

6 clicks intro

Lullaby

Fits with *Lullaby* in Brass, Woodwind and Percussion books (page 14)

O little town of Bethlehem

Fits with *O little town of Bethlehem* in Brass, Woodwind and Percussion books (page 49)

This melody can also be used with the accompaniment part in Team Strings book 1 (page 45)

3 clicks intro

Traditional

Upper F

Scale and arpeggio of F major

Little boy blue

Traditional

With a lilt

p

Fight the good fight

JOHN L. HATTON (1808–1886)

Brightly

f

Liza Jane

Traditional

4 clicks intro

Breezily

f

9

Pentatonic improvisation

Question and answer
Using the pentatonic scale on D

I know the Lord's laid his hands on me

7 clicks intro

Traditional

Caribbean dance

7 clicks intro

Traditional

The key of B♭ major

The notes E♭ and Upper E♭

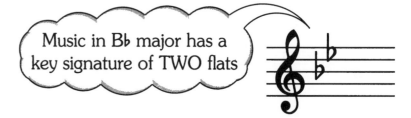

Music in B♭ major has a key signature of TWO flats

(4)

Scale and arpeggio of B♭ major (low)

John Brown's body

Traditional

Scale and arpeggio of B♭ major (high)

 Little donkey

Fits with *Little donkey* in Brass, Woodwind and Percussion books (page 37)

Words and Music by ERIC BOSWELL

4 clicks intro

1.

2.

3.

Pomp and circumstance

EDWARD ELGAR (1857–1934)

Blowin' in the wind

Fits with *Blowin' in the wind* in Brass, Woodwind and Percussion books (page 21)

Words and Music by BOB DYLAN

4 clicks intro

Third position

The magic carpet

Fits with *The wizard* in Team Strings book 1 (page 43)

Etude

The notes high C#
and high D

High C#

High D

Pease pudding hot

Moderately

Traditional

Scale and arpeggio of D major (2 octaves)

Song and dance

Fits with *Song and dance* in Team Strings book 1 (page 26)

Bright and rhythmic

Traditional

The key of A major

Music in A major has a
key signature of THREE sharps

Low C#

Row, row, row the boat

Round

Traditional

Flowing

mf

Shortnin' bread

4 clicks intro

Traditional

Crisply

The note G♯

Scale and arpeggio of A major
(2 octaves)

All made up

Victorian ballad

Auld lang syne

4 clicks intro

Traditional

Hoe down

4 clicks intro

Molly Wicks and the pupils
of Greenmeadow Junior School

1.

2.

3.

60

Key signature of
D minor

Scale and arpeggio of D minor harmonic
(2 octaves)

D minor round

The truth from above

3 clicks intro

Traditional

Charlie is my darling

Traditional

Scale and arpeggio of G minor harmonic
(2 octaves)

Key signature of G minor

Coventry carol

3 clicks intro

Traditional

Summertime

6 clicks intro

Music and Lyrics by GEORGE GERSHWIN, DUBOSE and DOROTHY HEYWARD and IRA GERSHWIN

Star wars

4 clicks intro

JOHN WILLIAMS

My heart will go on

Love theme from *Titanic*

Words by W. JENNINGS
Music by JAMES HORNER

4 clicks intro

Moderately

1.

Moderately

2.

Moderately

3.

Eternal Father, strong to save

3 clicks intro

Words by W. WHITING
Music by J.B. DYKES (1823–1876)

Smooth and flowing

Pink Panther

HENRY MANCINI